WHAT'S IT LIKE TO BE A...?

SPORTS TRAINER

Elizabeth Dowen   Lisa Thompson

Reprinted 2010
First published in the UK 2008 by
A & C Black Publishing Ltd
36 Soho Square
London
W1D 3QY
www.acblack.com

Copyright © 2008 Blake Publishing
Published 2007 by Black Education Pty Ltd, Australia

ISBN: 978-1-4081-0513-9

A CIP catalogue record for this book is available from the British Library.

Written by Lisa Thompson and Elizabeth Dowen
Publisher: Katy Pike
Series Editor: Eve Tonelli
Cover Design: Terry Woodley
Designer: D Brown
Printed in China by South China Printing Co. Ltd.

Cover image © Radius Images/PunchStock

Illustration credits: p21 (tl)-Shutterstock

This book is produced using paper made from wood grown in managed,
sustainable forests. It is natural, renewable and recyclable. The logging and
manufacturing processes conform to the environmental regulations of the
country of origin.

All the Internet addresses given in this book were correct at the time of
going to press. The author and publishers regret any inconvenience caused
if addresses have changed or sites have ceased to exist, but can accept no
responsibility for any such changes.

Contents

THAT WINNING FEELING!

I am courtside watching Shaun playing for his basketball team. He is one of my clients. It's a very close game and Shaun's team is only a few points behind. Suddenly, Shaun intercepts the ball. I quickly glance up at the clock — there are literally only seconds remaining in the game. If Shaun keeps his cool, his team has a chance of winning.

Shaun races down the side, playing the ball just like we practised in our training sessions. He looks relaxed and focused — I can tell he's in the zone. He leaps up and takes the shot. It's his only chance. He scores! It's a three pointer! The crowd goes wild! I go wild! The full-time siren sounds. It's all over.

All sports are good for you

Sports, such as basketball, develop self-esteem, encourage self-discipline and create confidence.

Shaun's team has won! They are ecstatic. This win means they have a chance of winning the Regional School Basketball Championships.

As Shaun's sports trainer, my mind is already going over the game and the recovery and training that's ahead of us. The win is all the more exciting because I've been training Shaun since he began recovery from a serious leg injury. Some experts thought he would never play again.

DID YOU KNOW?

Over the next five years Sport England expect a big increase in jobs within the coaching sector. A large part of the demand for coaches is expected in the education sector. Sportscoach UK, the lead body in coaching, aim to increase the number of people who coach professionally. 80% of the coaches in the UK are volunteers.

Opportunities in careers related to sport are increasing, especially with London hosting the 2012 Olympic and Paralympic games.

Stretching prepares your muscles for exercise.

Coaches decide tactics and strategies during the game.

cycling

After the game, I listen to the coach as he explains the training schedule for the next few weeks. When everybody has settled down and absorbed the win, I talk to Shaun and discuss our training plans for the weeks ahead. I want 100 percent focus and commitment. I want to keep Shaun motivated and positive. I know he has what it takes to fulfil his dream of being picked as a professional basketball player sometime in the near future.

circuit workout

As a sports trainer, I look after athletes and people interested in improving their fitness and recovery levels.

I pack up and head off after the game to see another of my Saturday clients for a one-on-one training session. It's going to be a busy afternoon but I'm on a high after watching Shaun's team win.

track workout

Understanding what's best

Sports coaches and trainers need to understand what's best for their clients. They encourage clients to work out at an effective level to help them achieve their goals. Many people need only one session to get on the right track, while others need longer and are only motivated to work hard under the watchful eye of a sports trainer.

triathlon

Evan's Diary

Saturday

12 pm Rick — amateur cyclist. meet at gym for circuit training workout.

2 pm Lisa — mum training to compete in her first marathon. meet at park for drills and stretching workout.

4:30 pm Greg — professional triathlete. meet at the pool, talk with swimming coach after his training, and then go to track to work on running and bike.

marathon

WHAT DOES A SPORTS TRAINER DO?

I help athletes achieve and maintain their fitness levels and increase their skills. I also help them prevent, or manage, injuries through exercise and recovery. Coaches, trainers and instructors are often concerned with one particular sport. We work with people of all ages, at every level, including those who are learning the sport for fun. Trainers who work with top professional sportspeople usually devise their training programmes and monitor their performance. It's my job to help athletes perform at their best, and to make sure they're in good shape and ready to play.

Many of the exercises I get my clients to do involves exercising in a way that prevents injuries. I lead teams and individuals through stretching exercises prior to each event, during practice and at the end of each event.

I also monitor small injuries and work out the best ways to deal with them and the recovery. If an athlete's hurt, I'm often the first one on the scene to determine the seriousness of the injury. I work with doctors and physiotherapists to set up training and exercise routines for an athlete's recovery programme.

DID YOU KNOW?

AVOIDING INJURY

There are a few simple steps you can take to avoid injury. Always wear the proper equipment when practising. In many sports, such as hockey and cricket, helmets are very important, as are shin guards, wrist pads and gloves. Wear proper footwear to cushion the feet — not too tight or too loose. Footwear should also provide support for the foot's arch.

increasing strength by using weights

stretching before a work out to warm up

8

starting young

protective gear

How I became a sports trainer

Gloves keep hands safe from injury.

I've been interested in sport since primary school where I was involved in swimming, basketball and football. I competed competitively for my school, but mostly I was into sport for fun.

As a teenager, I took up triathlons — a combination of swimming, cycling and running. While I was never an Olympic champion I always went out, no matter what the sport, and gave it my best.

fun run

I made a lot of friends playing sport. Even though I was very competitive I had fun — win, lose or draw — though nothing beats the high of winning.

At school I did A levels, including biology. Then I went to university and studied physical education. As part of the course, I studied sports science and did lots of courses relating to coaching and sports training.

While at university, I was still competing in triathlons. I began to write my own programmes as a way to try out some of the things I was learning. It was also a way of improving my performance. In fact, I improved so much in one season, other athletes on campus began asking me to write their programmes. Eventually, I was offered a job training the university rowing team.

Running is lots of fun and is a very effective way of keeping fit.

rowing

food science

physiology

All sports coaches need to understand how to nurture the skills that help make a winning sports team or individual. When I finished university I was lucky enough to have the contacts and experience to become an elite performance trainer. While most of my clients are professional athletes, where every second or centimetre of improvement counts, I also train everyday people who are interested in improving or maintaining their fitness.

Sports trainer core competencies are:

working with children and young people

sports nutrition

drugs in sport

principles of injury management

medical conditions affecting athletes

warm-up/cool-down and stretching exercises.

chemistry

Sports trainer subjects

Anatomy — understanding the structure and make-up of the body

Physiology — understanding how living organisms function

Food Science — studying all aspects of food, from harvesting to consumption — including nutrition and diet

First Aid and Health and Safety — studying the emergency care given to an injured person before medical aid can be obtained

Biology — scientific study of living organisms

Chemistry — the study of matter and its interactions.

Improving and Developing Performance

Coaching Process and Practice — including coaching strategies

Motivation and Behaviour Change

biology

first aid

WHAT MAKES A WINNING SPORTS TEAM OR INDIVIDUAL?

Things to keep in mind if you want to be a sports trainer:

Physical training

Winning attitude

Nutrition

Talent

Technique

MUST HAVE A LOVE OF SPORT

Have the ability and perseverance to search for solutions

BE DISCIPLINED

BE ETHICAL.

Be patient and understanding

Be positive and motivated

Be a good communicator

Running on grass is kinder to the body.

Knowing your stuff

Sports trainers need to keep up with new developments in sports science so they can best advise their clients. For example, recent research recommends running on grass rather than concrete or sand, as grass is easier on the body's joints and is less likely to cause injury.

Workplaces

Sports trainers work in a variety of settings with individuals and teams. Trainers may work in sport clubs, gyms, health clubs, small and large leisure centres, outdoor pursuit centres, schools, universities and spas. The work environment can be as individual as the trainers themselves.

Zomas

During the early Olympics, athletes wore loincloths called zomas. But, as the story goes, in 720 BC an athlete named Orsippus let his zoma fall so he could run more easily. From that time on, athletes competed completely naked (hence the word gymnasium, from the Greek word, *gymnos*, meaning naked).

Instructing and coaching can be a part-time job combined with another career. Some instructors build up enough part-time work, with a range of clubs or organisations, to create a full-time workload. Larger sports clubs and leisure centres, which have a high level of customer demand, may employ specialist fitness instructors, trainers or coaches on a full-time basis. The majority of coaching within the UK, however, is done on a voluntary basis; this can provide a good starting point from which to build up experience.

YOU'LL NEED GOOD COMMUNICATION SKILLS AND BE ABLE TO WORK WELL IN A TEAM. EVERYONE WORKING IN SPORT NEEDS TO BE AWARE OF HEALTH AND SAFETY ISSUES. FOR MANY JOBS, WORK TAKES PLACE AT WEEKENDS AND IN THE EVENINGS – WHEN OTHERS ARE ENJOYING TIME OFF!

Be prepared to work long and irregular hours

13

Other career options

There are other careers that relate to sports training that you may find interesting.

SPORTS AND LEISURE CENTRE STAFF

Depending on your experience you may be responsible for:

- looking after equipment and demonstrating how to use it safely
- assisting at classes and fitness sessions
- dealing with bookings and enquiries.
- planning sports and exercise programmes
- organising publicity and events
- dealing with rotas, recruitment and training
- overseeing health and safety
- managing other facilities and maintenance

In sports and leisure centres there are assistant and management positions available.

SPORTS MEDICINE AND PHYSIOLOGY

Doctors, physiologists and scientists are involved in research into the biology of exercise and fitness. There are opportunities in research, as consultants to national teams, for example, and there are teaching opportunities in places where subjects like sports science are taught.

PHYSIOTHERAPY AND SPORTS THERAPY

Physiotherapists treat injured sportspeople with methods like massage, electrical treatments, and water therapy. They advise on exercise routines, correct ways of using the body in training, and so on. There are qualifications in massage, offered by a number of professional bodies, which allow you to work in private clubs and fitness centres.

Dietician

Dieticians understand and research the science of food (vitamins, minerals, food groups) to help people select the right food combinations to gain, maintain and promote health.

SPORTS DEVELOPMENT WORKER

The purpose of the job is to:
- improve the public image of sport
- increase numbers involved in sport
- improve facilities available
- raise standards of achievement.

You may have to deal with funding and sponsorship, and organise promotional events or community schemes to encourage participation in sports.

PROFESSIONAL SPORTS

Most top professionals have a genuine talent for their sport and have been playing, and competing seriously, from a very early age. It is difficult to earn any money from competing and there tend to be fewer opportunities for women than men.

Keep your options open and take your education and training as far as you can.

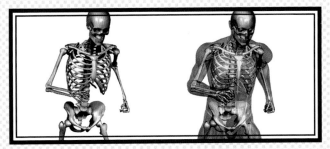

OUTDOOR PURSUITS AND EXTREME SPORTS

Instructors in a range of outdoor pursuits and extreme sports are employed by outdoor activity centres owned by local authorities or by private companies. Having recognised instructors' qualifications is very important, and teaching qualifications may be needed for some posts.

UMPIRES, REFEREES, JUDGES AND OTHER SPORT OFFICIALS

They observe the play and enforce the rules of the sport. They also impose penalties if the rules are broken. These officials are often required to make decisions in a split second.

Understanding the body

Understanding the human body enables sports coaches to write training programs and identify, evaluate and treat sport injuries. An understanding of the skeletal system, joints and ligaments, muscles and their attachments and the cardio-respiratory system (the heart and lungs) is essential.

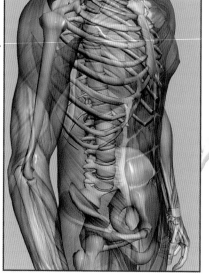

The skeletal system

There are 206 bones in the human body, many of which are connected through a variety of joints, allowing movement in multiple directions.

For an athlete, it is important that these joints are protected correctly to prevent injury and minimise wear and tear.

Back sprain is a common sport injury.

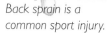

DIDYOUKNOW?

MUSCLE GAIN

Evolution has taught the body to carry just enough muscle to comfortably perform daily routines. This makes it very difficult to increase muscle mass. Also, any gained muscle is very easy to lose once exercise is stopped for any length of time. To increase their muscle mass, athletes need to work out with weights regularly.

Muscle groups

One of the ways athletes can protect their joints and bones is by building and toning muscles.

Skeletal muscles usually work in pairs, so a trainer must know a muscle's opposite muscle when working out a program to achieve maximum muscle balance, strength and stability.

Lifting weights helps build muscles.

If one muscle is overworked at the expense of another, it may leave an athlete vulnerable to injury. Training opposite muscle groups is also one way a trainer helps an athlete recover from injury.

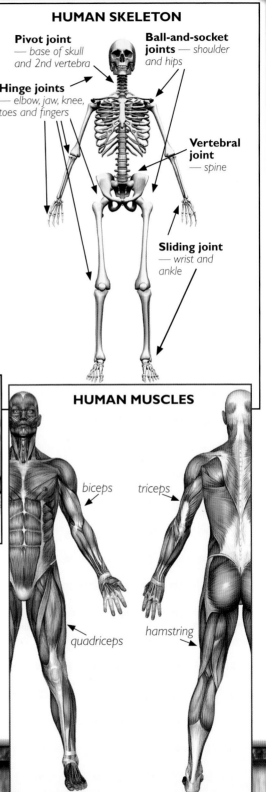

HUMAN SKELETON

Pivot joint — *base of skull and 2nd vertebra*

Ball-and-socket joints — *shoulder and hips*

Hinge joints — *elbow, jaw, knee, toes and fingers*

Vertebral joint — *spine*

Sliding joint — *wrist and ankle*

HUMAN MUSCLES

biceps

triceps

quadriceps

hamstring

THE TWITCH ADVANTAGE

Muscles are made up of fast and slow twitch fibres. Everyone has the same number of fibres in each muscle, although the proportion of fast to slow twitch varies from person to person.

Fast twitch fibres contract very quickly and yield a short burst of energy. They are used whenever a sudden show of speed or strength is made, such as sprinting. Slow twitch fibres are used more in endurance sports, such as distance running.

Scientists believe that successful sprinter muscles are 70 per cent fast twitch fibre. This compares to 50 per cent for the average person. This characteristic enables sprinters to explode out of the starting blocks with more speed and power.

Built for speed – could you outrun a cheetah?

An Olympic runner's maximum speed is 43.4 km/h, while the cheetah clocks 114.3 km/h. How does the cheetah move so fast? It's all in the cheetah's supple spine which bends like a spring as the animal runs. This enables the cheetah to bring its hind legs well forward of its front legs on each leap. At the beginning of the next leap, the spine straightens out, providing extra thrust to its strong hind legs.

The cheetah is the fastest of all land animals.

Fascinating facts about muscles

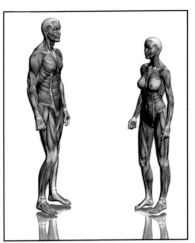

- There are approximately 650 skeletal muscles in the human body.

- About 40% of your weight is muscle.

- Your muscles are 75% water, 20% protein. The other 5% is a combination of salts, minerals and carbohydrates.

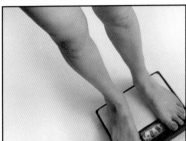

- For their size to strength ratio, the muscles that operate the wings of bees, flies and mosquitoes are stronger than any human muscles.

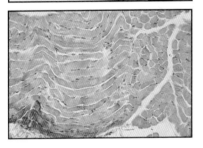

- One of the smallest muscles in the human body has one of the longest names. The *levator labii superioris alaeque nasi* is the tiny muscle beside your nose that raises your lip into a sneer.

A high percentage of fast twitch fibre helps with speed.

Built for sport

Human beings can be grouped into three basic body shapes: round, muscular, and lean and long. Everyone is a mixture of all three in different proportions. Certain sports favour particular body shapes — tall basketball players, hefty footballers, slight gymnasts. Your body shape may make you more suited to one particular sport. Your combination may also affect the amount of muscle mass you can build, and the type of fitness programme you need to stay in shape.

Being tall is useful for basketball players.

DIDYOUKNOW?

CESTUS

Cestus was a spectator sport in ancient Rome. Slaves fought to the death wearing spike-covered gloves. These gloves were the ancient equivalent of knuckle dusters or brass knuckles. Cestus became increasingly bloody until it was officially banned in the 1st century BC. Hand-to-hand fighting was banned in 393 AD.

It helps to be stocky for games such as rugby.

It's a definite advantage for female gymnasts to be slim and lean.

THE BODY TYPE CHART

Endomorphs — round

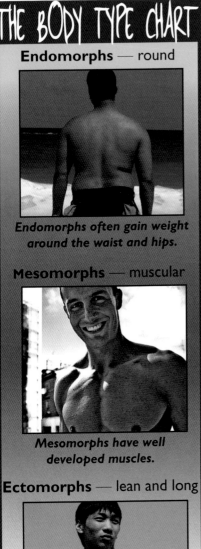

Endomorphs often gain weight around the waist and hips.

Mesomorphs — muscular

Mesomorphs have well developed muscles.

Ectomorphs — lean and long

Ectomorphs tend to be slim and sometimes underweight.

WORKING OUT AN ATHLETE'S BODY TYPE FORMULA

Sports scientists use specialised equipment to scientifically measure athletes for height, weight, length, width, circumference and fat.

The athletes are then assigned a rating from 1 to 7 for the amount of each component in their body mix, 1 being the lowest and 7 being the highest.

The athlete is then given a three-digit number, for example, 6-4-2. This means that on the endomorph scale they are a 6, on the mesomorph a 4 and on the ectomorph, they are a 2.

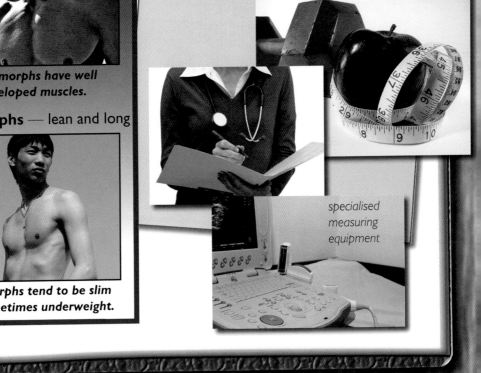

specialised measuring equipment

Timetable of a typical day

strength = speed

6:30 am-8 am — meet Rick (a client) at the gym. He is a cyclist. I am doing a weights programme with him to increase his strength. We also work on his mental focus, and proper technique on the stationary bike.

stationary bike

9 am — talk to a Pilates instructor about a client who wants to increase their core strength and flexibility without weights. Together, we devise a programme. Part of the challenge of being a sports trainer is constantly finding and trying out new ways for clients to achieve their fitness goals.

Pilates increases core strength.

10 am — meet Lisa, who's training for a marathon. We train for 90 minutes doing grass running in the local park.

Lisa prepares to get going.

Week 4: DAY 2

1:30 pm-4 pm — answer emails at the office, update training and recovery programmes, and monitor training and fitness results that have come in. Part of being a trainer is the need to assess both your own progress and the results of your clients. I organise some notes for a talk I am giving to a school about the importance of fitness and proper training in sport.

5 pm — meet Shaun at the basketball courts to go over some drills. We then do some stretching and speed work.

Shaun practising shooting

6 pm-7 pm — meet with a new client whose goal is to prepare for the ski season. The hour-long session includes interval and light strength training. Special emphasis is placed on balance training with trek poles that act like ski poles. I show the client how to use the stability ball for abdominal exercises and stretching. We go through the fitness plan I've drawn up for him and arrange to meet again in a week's time.

skiing

Wake up! Early starts are very common.

Client fills out health questionnaire.

Client's weight is checked regularly.

Before writing a programme, I need a client to do some basic tests to assess their fitness.

A fitness assessment lets me know their baseline fitness. It also gives us something to compare to, so we can monitor progress. This allows us to see which areas need to be worked on more and those showing the most improvement.

Fitness tests get to the heart of the matter.

HEART RATE

The heart is the body's strongest muscle. It pumps blood through the body. Every beat is recorded as a pulse.

The heart supplies more blood to an exercising muscle, and the harder an athlete works, the higher the pulse rate. A trainer can use an athlete's resting heart rate and maximum heart rate to see if they're working hard enough, or too hard, and plan a programme accordingly.

circulatory system

24

HOW TO RECORD YOUR RESTING HEART RATE

The two most common places for recording heart rate are the wrist and the neck.

1. Using two fingers, find a pulse and count the number of beats for 10 seconds. Multiply the number of beats by six.
2. This gives your heart beats per minute.
3. You need to record your heart beat before exercise (resting heart rate) and then right after your workout (maximum heart rate).

MEASURING MAXIMUM HEART RATE

1. Find a stable seat or bench.
2. Begin stepping up on the seat one leg at a time — using the opposite leg to come down on.
3. Continue doing this for five minutes.
4. After five minutes, record your heart rate.

Your maximum heart rate after exercise should be 220 beats per minute minus your age. This gives an indication of how hard you've been working and how fit you are. The lower your heart rate, the fitter you are. If your heart rate is noticeably high, or higher than the maximum, consider seeking medical advice from a doctor.

finding pulse on the wrist

printout of heart rate

finding pulse on the neck

Step up!

Keep it up for five minutes.

FLEXIBILITY TEST

1. Sit on the floor with your legs and feet straight out in front of you.
2. Bend forward towards your toes.
3. See how far you can reach.
4. Measure the distance. How far can you stretch?

All trainers and coaches need to have a basic first aid certificate. Some sports require higher levels of sports coaching accreditations. Having recognised instructor's qualifications is very important and some jobs also require a teaching qualification. The UK Coaching Certificate (UKCC) scheme has endorsed the coaching qualifications for 13 sports – this ensures that quality standards have been met.

SPEED

FLEXIBILITY

Working out a training programme

To write a training programme, as well as having an understanding of the base fitness of the person, I also need to know the athlete's training goals.

Fitness goals can be broken down into four key areas:

STAMINA
STRENGTH
SPEED
FLEXIBILITY.

Plan a programme accordingly.

STAMINA

STRENGTH

Stop when an injury occurs.

Apply ice wrapped in cloth to injury.

Bandage wound.

BASIC FIRST AID

The best response to an injury such as a sprain, twist or bad bruise is RICER. It is best to avoid heat, running, alcohol and massage. RICER is best done as soon as possible after injury.

Rest — rest from the activity causing injury.

Ice — apply ice to the wound. Ice limits swelling, which is important as swelling slows down the healing process. Wrap the ice in a cloth or a towel and place it on the injury.

Compression — compression also limits swelling. Apply a firm, elastic, non-adhesive bandage or plastic wrap. If using an ice pack, the compression bandage is applied over the ice pack and above and below the injury site to hold it in place and provide additional compression.

Elevation — raise the leg or arm higher than chest level. Gravity helps by preventing too much fluid from accumulating in the wound.

Refer and Record — refer to an appropriate health care professional for definitive diagnosis and continuing management. Record your observations, assessment and initial management before referral, and send a copy with the athlete to the professional.

Different types of exercise

Sports can be broken down into two different energy types: aerobic and anaerobic. Most sports are a combination of both.

aerobic exercise

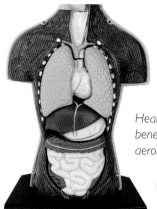
Heart and lungs benefit from aerobic exercise.

Aerobic

Aerobic literally means 'with air'. Aerobic exercise requires oxygen to produce rapid muscle movement. It is any exercise performed at a moderately high level of intensity over a long period of time, while maintaining an increased heart rate. The heart and lungs work together to supply oxygen to the body's tissues. Aerobic exercise strengthens the heart and lungs by forcing them to work harder.

Aerobic exercises include cycling, swimming, jogging, tennis, basketball and skiing. A typical session lasts anywhere from 20–60 minutes. Aerobic exercise immediately increases the body's metabolic rate (the amount of energy used) to between five and 20 times. Done regularly this change is very healthy.

Benefits

Aerobic exercise strengthens the heart, making it more efficient, thus lowering the risk of heart attack. It also places stress on the bones, which helps increase bone strength. It increases endurance by one-third or more, and enhances blood flow to the limbs and organs.

Anaerobic

Anaerobic means 'without air'. Anaerobic exercise is any exercise that requires short bursts of power, such as weight-lifting. A significant increase in oxygen is not needed to perform these exercises. Glycogen, a form of sugar, stored in the muscle is used when performing anaerobic exercise. Because this energy supply is limited, anaerobic exercise can only be sustained for short periods.

Benefits

Anaerobic exercise helps with sports performance and increases lean muscle mass.

anaerobic exercise

Regular aerobic exercise helps prevent heart attacks.

DIDYOUKNOW?

BASKETBALL — AN AEROBIC AND ANAEROBIC EXERCISE

In basketball, a player running back and forth across the court operates aerobically with occasional bursts of anaerobic energy for every jump shot or run at the basket.

Sports nutrition

FOOD is fuel. To compete at your best, you need to eat a healthy, balanced diet. I try to inspire all my clients to eat properly before and after events. I remind them that regardless of how much they train, or how dedicated they are, they will not perform at their best unless they give their bodies essential nutrients.

Three types of food provide energy – carbohydrates, protein and fat.

healthy diet

carbohydrates

Carbohydrates are everyone's major fuel source. Sports dieticians recommend that complex carbohydrates such as breads, cereals, fruits, vegetables and legumes (peas, beans, lentils) make up more than half our energy intake.

Carbohydrates are stored as glycogen in the muscles and liver. Muscles use glycogen as the main source of energy during exercise. When glycogen stores are used up exhaustion occurs.

Protein

Protein is essential for the growth and repair of all body tissues. Athletes have slightly higher protein needs because of wear and tear on their bodies. High-protein foods include beef, tuna, chicken, oats and cottage cheese.

DID YOU KNOW?

Iron

Iron is an important mineral for transporting oxygen around the body. Iron deficiency causes fatigue, as it reduces the amount of oxygen reaching the muscles. An adequate intake is vital for athletes to maintain performance. Oysters, red meat, spinach and treacle are examples of iron-rich foods.

fat

Fat has over twice the energy values of carbohydrates or protein. A small amount of fat is important in aiding the absorption and transportation of certain vitamins around the body. We all need dietary fat daily — a tablespoon is usually enough. Good fats tend to be liquid at room temperature (eg olive oil), while unhealthy fats are usually solid at room temperature (eg lard).

Sports nutrition

Glycaemic Index

The Glycaemic Index (GI) is a ranking which measures the effect of food on blood-sugar levels over two hours after the food is eaten.

Very high glucose (sugar) levels after meals are bad for general health as they damage the arteries and various blood vessels. They also promote high insulin levels which can lead to chronic illnesses, such as diabetes (a condition in which blood sugar levels are above normal which can damage blood vessels and nerves). Eating low-GI foods means avoiding high glucose levels, and supplies a much steadier stream of energy. This reduces the risk of heart disease and diabetes.

A glucometer is used to measure blood sugar levels.

LOW GI
(EAT PRIOR TO SPORT EVENT)

- baked beans
- brown bread
- pasta
- porridge
- long grain white rice
- muesli
- milk
- yoghurt
- most fruits

MODERATE GI – HIGH GI
(EAT AFTER SPORT EVENT)

- muesli bars
- rice bubbles
- cornflakes
- brown rice
- melon
- pita bread
- crumpet
- baked potato
- white bread
- sports drinks
- pumpkin

DIDYOUKNOW?

Dehydration and exercise

An average person may lose as much as 1 L to 1.9 L of fluid during one hour of exercise. When you are not drinking enough fluids, your muscles quickly tire and you may develop leg cramps. Always remember to drink more than your daily requirement of water before, during and after exercise.

33

TRAINING A WINNING MIND

A winning mind is the ability to maintain focus, control emotions and work effectively. This mindset can make the difference between winning and losing. Often the key to achieving peak performance is managing your emotional state.

persistence

enthusiasm

THE WINNING MENTAL QUALITIES OF CHAMPIONS

Desire — you want your goal so badly, you won't stop until you achieve it.

Enthusiasm and passion — passion and purpose equals motivation.

Determination and persistence — staying focused on the goal, even when losing.

Concentration — the ability to focus on the task at hand.

Confidence — the quiet assurance that you can, and will, win.

Positive attitude — positive desire and self-belief.

Courage — courage is not the absence of fear, but it's feeling the fear and doing it anyway.

Self-awareness — understanding the signals from your body and mental state, and allowing yourself time to rest, relax and sleep.

determination

THE ZONE IN SPORT

THE ZONE IN SPORT

The zone is a mental state of calmness and confidence where the athlete is totally in the here-and-now. There is total focus, and actions and decisions seem effortless and easy.

MODELLING

MODELLING

The secret to becoming good at something quickly is MODELLING.

Modelling is finding out how somebody does something, and then adopting and adapting their approach to suit your own purposes.

So you want to be the best? Then study champions and copy them.

You can save yourself years of practice by studying how someone else does something and then borrowing their approach.

In the zone

See how the professionals do it.

courage

replaying the point

studying the competition

Sports training and coaching tips

To be an effective sports trainer you need to be a good leader. Leaders are people who can motivate, guide and direct others to give their best. Leaders are made through discipline, training, experience and the desire to continually improve. Here are some tips on how to be a good leader.

Learn to be strong but not rude

It is important to stay relaxed and friendly when leading others. Being a trainer can be stressful, but good trainers know how to stay relaxed and get their message across.

Understand your client or team members

Understand what really motivates them. Care enough to see if there's anything holding them back or preventing them from achieving their best. Always remember, praise is one of the greatest motivators of all.

Set goals

Achieving goals is a great motivator. It's also helpful to break a big dream into small achievable steps.

Never pass negatives down

Focus on successes rather than failures. Build on strengths rather than weaknesses.

Develop humour

Always remember that sport is meant to be fun!

Lead by example

Use the right mental techniques so you can teach the importance of the mind in sport. Show clients how to stay positive, overcome defeat and manage emotions. Use visualisation techniques to teach new skills and improve drills.

SHAUN'S TRAINING COUNTDOWN
-BEHIND THE SCENES

Two days after the game, Shaun and I meet. We watch the game on video and look at areas where Shaun could have done better, and the things he did that were great (like shoot the winning points!). Shaun is still motivated by the win, and it shows in his eagerness to train.

watching footage of the game

Shaun's goals this training session: to increase his speed and agility and to stay focused while practising ball skills.

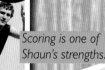
Scoring is one of Shaun's strengths.

We begin our session with warming up exercises. Warming up is a must, especially if you are coming back from an injury. While warming up, I get Shaun to focus and concentrate on his goals for this training session.

Focus on the goal.

practising ball skills

We spend 30 minutes going over basic ball skills, handling, passing and dribbling. To be the best basketball guard possible, Shaun needs to have these skills down so well they are second nature. This will help him achieve moments were he is in the zone like the last game. Being good at the game's simplest skills makes the more difficult moves easier.

protecting the ball

Speed on court is essential for success.

We do speed and quickness drills with the ball. I get Shaun to think about being ball quick as basketball is a game of speed and agility.

We concentrate on Shaun protecting the basketball. Shaun concentrates on keeping control of the ball. He can pass it high and soft or fast and low and change the speed of a ball in a second. His first dribble can look weak and his second look strong.

knees bent, dribbling low

long jump in the Ancient Olympics

DIDYOUKNOW?

What's in a word?

Athlos is the ancient Greek word for contest. Competitors were called athletes.

We practise game tactics and playing speed as these will help Shaun outperform others. We spend 10 minutes doing free throw shooting — Shaun must make 12 shots in a row before the session is over. We end with more stretches. Shaun and I meet twice more before the championships.

By the time the big game arrives, Shaun and his team are determined to win.

practising free throw shooting

Shaun really wants to win!

tactics for the big game

THE BIG DAY ARRIVES

The roar of the crowd is deafening. I wonder if Shaun even notices the crowd. I've never seen him play with such a burning desire to win. His focus and determination have motivated the rest of his team, keeping them in front by one point.

It's a fast, tight game and everyone's tired. But Shaun has remembered the tactics we practised, and the speed and the attitude of the ball change when he gains control. He still has energy. His team has noticed that if they get the ball to Shaun they are virtually guaranteed to get it down their end.

Shaun intercepts the ball and gains control. He dribbles it low and controls the game's speed. He plays with the defence as he waits for one of his team to get clear and take a shot. Suddenly, he sees a break and throws the ball high and long. His team-mate explodes into a high jump and flicks the ball into the basket.

ancient ball court in Tikal, Guatemala

DID YOU KNOW?

POK-TAPOK

Pok-tapok was an ancient ball game that was played in Central America several thousand years ago. The ball was made of rubber and filled with sacred plants. Only the hips, thighs and knees could touch it. The object of the game, which was played on a court, was to hit the ball into one of two goals which were flat stone slabs with a hole cut through the centre.

The crowd roars to its feet. The other team breaks in defeat. I notice two selectors on the other side to the stadium busily pointing at players and discussing them. Shaun's team has won, and it looks like Shaun is one step closer to being selected for the elite and competitive world of professional basketball.

Being part of the journey to people achieving their dreams and tasting sports victory is one of the greatest rewards of being a sports trainer.

Apprenticeships for sports trainers

You can start training with an employer through an Apprenticeship in Active Leisure and Learning a title which can include instructing, activity leadership, spectator control and other areas of sports work.

Practise being your own sports trainer — NOW!

- Do your own fitness test.
- Set a goal to work towards.
- Find a training partner.
- Get out of your comfort zone — try something new.
- Learn about the human body and sport.
- Find a role model.
- Join a team or volunteer at a sports club.

Start a training diary

Date	Exercise	Duration	Ate/Drank	How I felt
12/10	Jog	30 mins	Banana/Water	Tired at start but felt energised after the run. In good mood afterwards.
14/10	Gym	60 mins	Muesli bar/Water	Feeling good to begin with. Tired a little during workout but felt great after.
17/10	Tennis	60 mins	Sports drink	Started really enthusiastically and managed to maintain this throughout game! Felt tired but satisfied afterwards.
18/10	Hockey	60 mins	Banana/Sports drink	After tennis yesterday, felt drained but as the game progressed got into it.
21/10	Jog	45 mins	Had porridge an hour before. Drank water before run.	Felt really energised and happy after this well-paced, lengthy run.

OTHER RELATED CAREER AREAS TO CONSIDER:

Sports development worker

You may need a higher education qualification, and to be a sports enthusiast. Previous experience of sports-related work, administrative experience or business training is very helpful.

Greenkeeping and grounds staff

at sports clubs, leisure centres and local parks.

Physiotherapy and sports therapy

Qualifying as a professional physiotherapist through a degree will lead to the widest employment opportunities. The International Institute of Sports Therapy and other bodies offer sports therapy qualifications.

Lifeguards and attendants

lifeguard qualifications are awarded by The Royal Lifesaving Society UK, The Swimming Teachers' Association or the Surf Life Saving Association.

Teaching PE in school

Entry to a teacher-training degree course requires two A levels, or the equivalent, plus GCSEs including maths and English at grades A*-C. Science GCSE at grade A*-C (or equivalent) is required for trainee primary school teachers.

Independent schools do not always require qualifications, and they often give sport a high priority. Larger independent schools may employ professional coaches who are not trained teachers, but experts in their sport.

DID YOU KNOW?

The FA aims to recruit around 10,000 referees a year, to make sure that every football game has a qualified official.

For those interested in finding out more about refereeing in football, rugby union and cricket, the following websites have more information:
www.thefa.com
– click on 'the FA' and then 'refereeing' on the left-hand side
www.rfu.com
– click on 'community rugby' then 'referee/officiate'
www.acus.org.uk
– click on 'training'

Sport as an interest

If these job ideas are not for you, remember that sport is a great hobby and activity for your free time. It is great for your health and provides teamwork skills. And most importantly – it's a lot of fun!

43

At 14-16:

You have several options to consider:

- GCSEs are available in Physical Education and sciences. Some schools offer a GCSE in leisure and tourism.
- Sports Leaders UK offers various sports leadership awards. These qualifications are suitable for volunteers, and they can be used as a stepping-stone to employment.
- By 2010 there will be a Specialised Diploma available in the UK in Sports and Leisure.

At 16-18:

- There are full-time courses, such as those leading to BTEC National in Sport - available in a range of specialisations including development; coaching and fitness; performance and excellence; and outdoor adventure.
- AS and A2 qualifications in Sports and Leisure provide broad introductions to the leisure industry as a whole.
- Some colleges may offer OCR National qualifications in Sport.
- The national governing bodies of most sports (for example, The Football Association) offer their own instructor qualifications, and these are required for most paid jobs. An NVQ in Sport, Recreation and Allied Occupations specialising in coaching, teaching and instructing is available – this is relevant to a variety of sports.
- Organisations like Sports Coach UK offer workshops, from introductory to advanced level.

s coach

Next Steps:

To be accepted onto a degree course you need two A levels, or equivalent, as well as supporting GCSEs. A science A level is specified for some courses. Foundation degrees and HNDs have more flexible entry requirements. If you have exceptional sporting talent (for example, national representation), you may find that entry requirements can be lowered. You need to check requirements of individual courses carefully, as they do vary.

At 18+

There are many degree, HND and foundation degree courses related to sport. Examples of course titles include Sports Science, Sports Studies, Sports Development, Coaching Science and Sports Management. Some courses focus on the science of sport, others on sports leadership in the community. There are a few courses related to particular sports, for example, football studies and golf management.
There are also a variety of courses related to recreation and leisure industry management.

Some colleges want candidates of county standard in their main sport, while others merely look for 'strong interest'. Some courses have scholarships and bursaries available for people with particular sporting talents. You need to ask admissions tutors for advice.

British Universities' Sports Association (BUSA) can provide information about institutions with particular strengths in particular sports.

Postgraduate courses related to sports and recreation include the PGCE – for people interested in working as PE teachers.

Useful contacts and websites

SkillsActive – Castlewood House, 77-91 New Oxford Street, London WC1A 1PX. Careers advice line: 08000 933300 (for information on NVQs, Apprenticeships and careers). The Sector Skills Council for active leisure and learning. *www.skillsactive.com*

British Universities' Sports Association – 20-24 King's Bench Street, London SE1 0QX. Tel: 020 7633 5080. *www.busa.org.uk*

CCPR (Central Council of Physical Recreation) – Burwood House, 14-16 Caxton Street, London SW1 0QT. Tel: 020 7854 8500. *www.ccpr.org.uk*

Sports Leaders UK – 23-25 Linford Forum, Rockingham Drive, Linford Wood, Milton Keynes MK14 6LY. Tel: 01908 689180. *www.sportsleaders.org*

Institute of Sport and Recreation Management – Sir John Beckwith Centre for Sport, Loughborough University, Loughborough LE11 3TU. Tel: 01509 226474. Information on jobs and courses can be found on: *www.isrm.co.uk*

Sports coach UK – 114 Cardigan Road, Headingley, Leeds LS6 3BJ. Tel: 0113 274 4802. *www.sportscoachuk.org*

UK Sport – 40 Bernard Street, London WC1N 1ST. Tel: 020 7211 5100. *www.uksport.gov.uk*

Sport England – 3rd Floor, Victoria House, Bloomsbury Square, London WC1B 4SE. Tel: 0845 8508 508. National and regional sporting contacts, including governing bodies of sports (click on 'Get resources' then 'Useful links') can be found on: *www.sportengland.org*

The British Association of Sport and Exercise Sciences – LMU, Carnegie Faculty of Sport and Education, Fairfax Hall, Headingley Campus, Beckett Park, Leeds LS6 3QS. Tel: 0113 283 6162. Website has a course finder and you can download A Guide to Careers in Sport & Exercise Sciences (click on 'Students' then 'Careers'): *www.bases.org.uk*

Glossary

amateur — athlete who is not paid for playing sport

baseline fitness — measure of a person's level of fitness before embarking on a training program

carbohydrates — sugars, starches and fibre, that are a major source of energy for humans

circuit training — form of training that involves moving quickly between many different exercise machines

cool down — light exercise and stretching which lessens muscle soreness — done after playing sport

dehydration — loss of fluids from the body

dribbling — act of bouncing a ball

ethics — set of moral values

gymnasium — place where athletic exercises are practised

insulin — chemical substance produced by the pancreas which controls the amount of sugar in the blood by moving it into the cells, where it can be used by the body for energy

ligament — band of tissue that connects or supports bones and joints

marathon — long distance event based on an ancient Greek event — run over a distance of just over 42 km

metabolic rate — rate at which food is converted into energy

minerals — nutrients needed by the body in small amounts to help it function properly and stay strong

Pilates — strength training movements involving coordinated breathing techniques, developed in Germany by Dr. Joseph Pilates during the 1920s

rehabilitation — returning an athlete to normal activities after injury

sprain — injury to a ligament due to tearing or stretching

stability ball — large inflated rubber ball used for exercises and rehabilitation

starting blocks — block providing support for a runner's feet at the start of a race

wakeboarding — combination of water skiing and surfing, where the rider is towed behind a boat

warming up — gradual warming of the muscles through light exercise which lessens the likelihood of injuries while playing sport

Index